To:

....

From:

....

60 DEVOTIONS INSPIRED BY
Women of the Bible

ZONDERVAN
BOOKS

60 Devotions Inspired by Women of the Bible

Portions of this book were adapted from *Beloved.*

Requests for information should be addressed to:
Zondervan, *3900 Sparks Dr. SE, Grand Rapids, Michigan 49546.*

Contributor: Lindsay A. Franklin
Cover design: Jamie DeBruyn
Interior design: Emily Ghattas

ISBN 978-0-310-15166-1 (softcover)
ISBN 978-0-310-15168-5 (audio)
ISBN 978-0-310-15167-8 (ebook)

Printed in the United States of America

23 24 25 26 27 LBC 5 4 3 2 1

Introduction

Women are bombarded by lots of different messages about who they're supposed to be—and often, those messages contradict each other. So, what's the right path? Who do we listen to? Which messages should be filtered out, and which should be embraced?

If we're followers of Jesus, we look to God's Word for answers. What does God think about the issues we face? What does he say about who we're supposed to be and how we're supposed to act? What does it mean to be a godly woman, anyway?

We can find a lot of wisdom about this in Proverbs 31. But is that all the Bible has to say about being a woman? Maybe you feel like your entire identity as a woman can't fit into a proverb. Welcome to the club, sister. Few of us feel like we can be summed up in a small sound bite.

Thankfully, the Bible has *so much more* to say about the unique challenges—the heartaches and the high points—of being female.

Examining the stories of the women who came before us, we'll discover role models and cautionary tales, tragedies and triumphs. The stories of these ancient women are surprisingly relevant to our lives today.

Your identity as a woman matters to God, beloved sister. So, let's see what he has to say about it.

Eve

"Adam named his wife Eve, because she would
become the mother of all the living."
—Genesis 3:20

E ve's name is derived from the Hebrew word *chavah*, mean-
ing "to breathe" or the related word *chayah*, "to live." Breath
and life. Eve alone of all women lived without sin for a time. She
experienced the fullness of God's favor and blessing. Only in understanding that can we fully appreciate the tragedy of her mistake.

Eve was deceived into disobeying God's one restriction (Genesis
3:5–6). Ever since, she has been defined by her mistake. Can you
imagine if your worst blunder, the offense you committed that you
were *most* ashamed of, echoed through millennia and became one
of the most important moments in redemptive history?

We may worry an embarrassing video will get posted to social
media and go viral. That would be bad enough. But being known
as "that woman who started sin" for all time is surely worse. And
yet, that's not the whole of who Eve was. Womankind was the

missing piece of the creation puzzle, and God fitted that piece perfectly through Eve. She was *that* before she was "the sin woman."

You are not defined by your mistakes, either, no matter how much it feels that way sometimes. God saw Eve as the complete person she was. She suffered consequences, absolutely, but God also blessed and cared for her. We don't have to let our mistakes become our identity.

Are there any mistakes in your past that you've inadvertently folded into your identity? Write out the ways God has redeemed those events of the past, and jot down some new adjectives about yourself to embrace in light of God's work.

....

....

....

....

....

....

....

....

....

Noah's Wife

"But I will establish my covenant with you, and
you will enter the ark—you and your sons and
your wife and your sons' wives with you."
—Genesis 6:18

It's not the most glamourous mention in the Bible. In fact, it's
easy to skip over. Noah's wife doesn't get a detailed, three-
dimensional rendering the way many other biblical women do. We
don't even get her name. While Noah is the star of the story about
the flood, it's important to remember his wife was alongside him
the whole time. So, in many ways, Noah's story is her story too.

The old saying "behind every great man is a great woman" was
probably true in Noah's case. He would have needed a lot of support to complete the task God had given to him! It probably took
Noah many years to build the ark, and his neighbors must have
thought he was crazy.

Noah and his family are a strong example of resisting the
evils of one's culture and finding favor with God rather than man.

Scripture shows us that mankind has gone morally astray many, many times before. And our world is likely to get worse before Jesus returns.

While that may sound depressing, we can find encouragement in the stories of people like Noah and his family. Noah found favor in God's eyes, and he and his family were rescued. Noah carried out the work God called him to—with the support of his wife, we presume—no matter what others might think.

Have you ever felt like you don't belong in your own culture? What are some of the ways God has encouraged you in those times when you felt like an outsider?

Sarah

"God also said to Abraham, 'As for Sarai your wife, you are no longer to call her Sarai; her name will be Sarah. I will bless her and will surely give you a son by her. I will bless her so that she will be the mother of nations; kings of peoples will come from her.'"
—Genesis 17:15–16

S arai had her name for many decades. She was probably pretty comfortable with it. And then God decreed her name would be Sarah instead of Sarai. Why? *Sarai* means "my princess" in Hebrew. Sarah is a similar name with the same root, but it has grander connotations—almost like "queen mother" or "mother of nations." A fitting change for the role God was asking Sarai to assume. She was going to be the mother of Abraham's promised miracle child—the mother of many nations to come.

We don't usually change our actual names, but our relationship with God does change our labels, and that's really what God was doing for Sarai. Think of who you used to be before you met Jesus.

What are some of the labels you ascribed to yourself before God began to change you into Christ's image?

Maybe you used to feel like a screw-up—like nothing you did was right—but now God has removed that label and shown you how loved you are. Or maybe you felt like everything you did was perfect, but now God has removed that label and replaced it with humility to show you places you need to grow. God is constantly remaking us in his image to glorify his name.

What are some labels God might want to replace for you so you can better fulfill his purpose in your life?

....

....

....

....

....

....

....

....

Hagar

"[Hagar] gave this name to the LORD who spoke to
her: 'You are the God who sees me,' for she said,
'I have now seen the One who sees me.'"
—Genesis 16:13

Hagar had a rough go. She was Sarai's maidservant, and
when Sarai doubted God's promise of a son, she gave Hagar
to Abram so they might produce an heir (quite disturbing to our
modern sensibilities). Tension arose between the women, and
Hagar fled from Sarai's abuse. That's where God spoke to her in
the wilderness, and Hagar responded with the words in this verse.

Have you ever felt misunderstood? Or maybe like no matter
how hard you try to relate to others, you're just on a different wave-
length than everyone else? It would probably be too ironic if I told
you, "You're not alone." But it's true. Many people feel that sting of
loneliness and invisibility. Some feel it more often than others, but
everyone has probably experienced it sometime.

But we have a God who sees us. He doesn't merely observe

our appearance. Our God *sees* us—our whole selves, from our outer appearance to our inner organs, minds, and hearts. Our very souls are not only seen but *understood* by God.

If you ever feel alone and lost like Hagar was, remember there is a God who sees you and everything you're going through. He is there to talk to, to comfort you, and to lead you toward your next step. You never need to feel like no one gets you. God does.

Do you ever feel misunderstood or invisible? Write out truths you know about God—*he sees me, he loves me, he understands who I am*—to encourage you the next time you feel lonely.

Lot's Wife

"Thus [God] overthrew those cities and the entire
plain, destroying all those living in the cities—
and also the vegetation in the land. But Lot's wife
looked back, and she became a pillar of salt."
—Genesis 19:25–26

Lot was Abraham's nephew, and God was merciful to Lot's family for Abraham's sake. They were hand-plucked from the middle of a doomed city and given a chance to escape. Abraham had begged for the city to be spared, but not even ten righteous people could be found in it. Still, God sent angels to make sure Abraham's family made it out safely.

But Lot's wife looked back, exactly as the angels had instructed them not to.

Oh, this hurts. Why did Lot's wife disobey? Why didn't she just run for her life with her husband and daughters? She was so close!

Jesus' comments shed some light. In Luke 17:32–33 he says to the disciples, "Remember Lot's wife! Whoever tries to keep their life will lose it, and whoever loses their life will preserve it." It seems Lot's wife was not merely glancing back but longing for her life in the city. And remember, the depths of wickedness in this city were so great, the Lord completely destroyed all who lived there. Perhaps the sharpest lesson from the story of Lot's wife's is to fight our longings for sin.

From time to time, we are all tempted, and our sin nature would seek to pull us down into a pit. But we can learn from Lot's wife and keep our eyes facing forward toward God and his holiness.

Do you struggle to keep your eyes focused forward, instead glancing back at the past, whether with longing or guilt? Write out some thoughts about the future Jesus has promised you.

Rebekah

"[Rebekah] said to him, 'My son, let the curse fall on me. Just do what I say; go and get them for me.'"
—Genesis 27:13

Rebekah—wife of Isaac, the promised son of Sarah and Abraham—was hatching quite a scheme here. She wanted Jacob, her favorite son, the younger of her twin boys, to get the blessing that actually belonged to his older brother, Esau. God had already said Jacob would be the father of his people, but that wasn't quite enough assurance for Rebekah. She wanted to be *really* certain Jacob would be blessed, so she resorted to tricking her husband.

Like Sarah before her, Rebekah seemed to want to take matters into her own hands to force God's promise to come true. That may sound a little silly, but how often are we guilty of the same? Sometimes we take hasty or unwise action to make sure we feel safe, loved, financially secure, or validated. We're not so different from these ancient women.

Friend, God doesn't need our help to keep his promises. He

doesn't need anything from us at all. What he *wants* is our trust and obedience. When we honor God with our trust in his words, he is glorified all the more when he stays true to his promises.

Do you feel like you sometimes try to force situations to make sure God's promises will come true? What are some ways you can release the need for control and increase your trust in God's words?

....

....

....

....

....

....

....

....

....

....

Rachel

> "Leah had weak eyes, but Rachel had a lovely
> figure and was beautiful."
> —Genesis 29:17

Jacob grew up and married two sisters, Leah and Rachel. Through these two women and their two maidservants, he fathered the twelve tribes of Israel. Marrying any two sisters sounds like a recipe for trouble, but this short, rather strange verse when we first meet Leah and Rachel hints at the tension that would start a war of childbearing and intense competition once Jacob married these particular sisters.

Rachel was "the pretty one." Ugh. If you have siblings, friends, or even coworkers with whom you are constantly compared, you know how hurtful descriptors like this can be. The pretty one. The successful one. The smart one. Rachel was the pretty sister, the loved wife, the favored one. Jacob wanted to marry her, and Leah got folded up in the deal.

Whenever we feel like we're compared to someone else and

found wanting, it can hurt. But we don't have to own the negative comparisons others foist upon us. We can choose to focus on our strengths, the wonderful things that God and others see when they look at us. We *all* have these qualities, and yet we're so prone to embracing the negative descriptors instead. Think about your positives today. Focus on embracing those God-given attributes.

Have you experienced an unfavorable comparison in your life that has stuck with you? Write out the wonderful qualities you see in yourself and others see in you to combat the lie that you're not enough.

Leah

"When the Lord saw that Leah was not loved, he enabled
her to conceive, but Rachel remained childless. Leah
became pregnant and gave birth to a son. She named
him Reuben, for she said, 'It is because the Lord has seen
my misery. Surely my husband will love me now.'"
—Genesis 29:31–32

Leah, girl, we hear you. God heard her too. Our Bible says Leah
was "not loved," but the Hebrew word (*sane*) literally means
"hated." Did Jacob actually hate Leah? Did he despise his own
wife? That's a sad thought! It's possible this Hebrew word is simply
trying to express that Leah was loved much less than Rachel. But
even if Jacob didn't have passionate feelings of hatred toward Leah,
one thing is sure—Leah was not a favored, treasured wife, and the
Lord saw her pain.

When we're not loved by others—especially those whose love
and attention we strongly desire—it cuts. Deeply. When we're
rejected by our parents, abandoned by a spouse, dropped by a

friend, or estranged from a child, the pain can be crushing. But no matter how unloved we are by those who should accept us, it doesn't change God's view of who we are. He isn't swayed by the value others place on us. God didn't look at Leah and see someone worthless just because Jacob failed to appreciate her.

Loving someone who doesn't love you back never feels good. But when we're confident that God values and adores us, it becomes easier to shrug off the rejection of others. Let's thank God for his boundless love—that we are seen and known and beloved.

Have you experienced rejection from a loved one? Who hurt you? How has your faith in God allowed you to overcome that hurt?

....

....

....

....

....

....

....

Dinah

"Now Dinah, the daughter Leah had borne to Jacob,
went out to visit the women of the land."
—Genesis 34:1

Among the twelve sons of Jacob, only one daughter is mentioned by name, and that's Dinah. Her story is horrifying, tragic, and controversial. In our English translations what happened to Dinah sounds like a clear case of sexual assault (Genesis 34:2–4). Her story was tragic.

In the past (and even today), some people have used Dinah's "going out" to suggest that whatever happened next was Dinah's fault, because she went out without her father or brothers by her side. In other words, they say Dinah was "asking for it." This ignores the many other women in the Bible who "went out" with no blame assigned to them or impropriety implied (Jael, Rachel, Rebekah, and Abigail, for example). But it reveals a strange human impulse that is still a problem today: victim-blaming.

When something terrible happens, the first question many

ask amounts to, "What did you do to cause it?" Not only does this make it very difficult for victims to feel safe coming forward, it heaps undue responsibility on a person already dealing with trauma. When we approach those who are suffering with compassion instead, we can better show the love of Jesus to them. That empathy can be life giving.

What is your first response when something bad happens? If you tend to point fingers, think through some compassionate statements and kind questions you might offer instead.

Potiphar's Wife

> "Now Joseph was well-built and handsome, and after a while his master's wife took notice of Joseph and said, 'Come to bed with me!'"
> —Genesis 39:6–7

Jacob's favorite son—Rachel's son Joseph—had been sold into slavery in Egypt by his brothers. But, despite his predicament, the Lord blessed Joseph, and he found favor with his master, Potiphar. Scripture says Potiphar so trusted Joseph, he "left everything he had in Joseph's care" (Genesis 39:6).

But then there was Potiphar's wife. She clearly did not have the trustworthiness of Joseph!

When we're reading about people from ancient, distant cultures in the Bible, it's easy to assume that women never had power. Generally speaking, they had much less freedom and control than men in their society. But here we have an example of a biblical woman who had all the power—and she was seeking to abuse it.

As modern women, we're likely to be in positions of power at some point in our lives. It might be in our jobs, our families, our communities, or even our government. And when we do find ourselves in a position of power, it's important that we *don't* do what Potiphar's wife did. Having power is a big responsibility, and we fail in that responsibility when we try to use our power selfishly. When in a position of authority, let's pray we'll remain humble and treat everyone with dignity and respect—especially those who are at a disadvantage.

In what areas of your life do you hold authority right now? Are you the head of a ministry at church, a manager of people at work, or perhaps raising children? How can you show those under your care respect and kindness?

....

....

....

....

....

....

....

Shiphrah & Puah

"The king of Egypt said to the Hebrew midwives, whose names were Shiphrah and Puah, 'When you are helping the Hebrew women during childbirth on the delivery stool, if you see that the baby is a boy, kill him; but if it is a girl, let her live.' The midwives, however, feared God and did not do what the king of Egypt had told them to do; they let the boys live."
—Exodus 1:15–17

A lot had happened since the days of Joseph and Potiphar's wife. The sons of Jacob, along with their large families, moved to Egypt, and that was the beginning of the nation of Israel—the Hebrew people.

But it didn't take long for the pharaoh to become threatened by this new nation-within-a-nation. So, he enslaved the Hebrews, and that brings us to Shiphrah and Puah.

Imagine the horror of this command they received. Their whole job was to bring life into the world, safely guiding babies and mothers through the childbirth process. But Pharaoh was the highest authority in the land. In fact, ancient Egyptians worshiped their kings as gods and viewed their pharaoh as a mediator between common people and the divine. We're supposed to obey our government . . . right?

Romans 13 and other passages do tell us to respect and obey the governments over us. But *not* at the expense of God's commands. Shiphrah and Puah had a choice to make. Which did they care more about, their fear of the king or their respect, love, and fear of God?

Thankfully, they chose what was right—they let the baby boys live. Shiphrah and Puah are an excellent example of when it's right to disobey the law of the land. They did so peacefully and in a way that preserved life rather than destroyed it.

Can you remember a time when you had to choose between obeying a command or honoring God's commands instead? If that hasn't happened to you personally, write out a prayer for those facing such choices daily.

....

....

....

....

....

Jochebed

"When the child grew older, [Jochebed] took him to
Pharaoh's daughter and he became her son. She named
him Moses, saying, 'I drew him out of the water.'"
—Exodus 2:10

Moses was among the Hebrew babies meant to be drowned in the Nile, but through the intervention of his mother, Jochebed; his sister (possibly Miriam); and Pharoah's daughter —all guided by God— Moses lived. His own mother nursed him, then he was handed over to the princess to be raised as her son.

How did this part of the story feel for Jochebed? Moses was her baby. She'd had the divinely planned opportunity to care for him in his early years. And then, Jochebed had to give her son to the princess. Since Moses' heritage wasn't a secret, it's possible he stayed connected to his community and family throughout his years in the palace. But even so, Jochebed made a great sacrifice to save her son's life.

It's not easy to let go like Jochebed did. She had some strong motivation—literally saving her son's life—but it was probably still hard to follow through. Most people like to have control, but God often asks us to trust *him*—to release control to one much bigger and greater than ourselves. It's a tall order for us. But when we remember that God has a plan, releasing our grip becomes a little easier. God sees the whole design and he knows what we need most (even when it's not what we *want* most). Trust in God's good plan for you!

Is it hard for you to release control in your life? Write out some of God's promises to help bolster your trust in him (e.g., God will never leave me; God wants good things for me).

Miriam

"I brought you up out of Egypt and redeemed
you from the land of slavery. I sent Moses to
lead you, also Aaron and Miriam."
—Micah 6:4

Miriam wasn't a perfect person. She was a woman who had an up-and-down journey. An honored leader and prophet (Exodus 15:20). A woman who let her arrogance cloud her judgment when she wrongly accused Moses of sinning (Numbers 12:1–2). A woman who was publicly disciplined (Numbers 12:9–12). A woman who was restored (Numbers 12:13–15). An artist immortalized in song (Exodus 15:1–18). Miriam was all of these things, and more.

But here in the book of Micah, hundreds of years after Miriam lived and God saved his people from Egypt, God once again honored Miriam by referring to her not as a person who made mistakes, but as a woman he sent, along with her brothers, to save his people from Egypt. It's a powerful redemption for this complex woman.

Her story didn't end with "she made a huge mistake, and God was angry with her."

We are all works in progress. Our stories are still being written. Sometimes, when difficult things happen in our lives, it can feel like this is our whole story, now and forevermore. Maybe we worry our stories are over. But God is always writing a new chapter. When we can't see the whole book, God nudges us to at least flip the page.

What sort of chapter are you writing in your life right now? Is it peaceful, joyous, challenging—perhaps unbearably difficult? Write out a prayer for your current chapter, including your hopes for what's to come when you flip the page.

....

....

....

....

....

....

....

....

Zelophehad's Daughters

"[The daughters of Zelophehad] stood before Moses, Eleazar the priest, the leaders and the whole assembly at the entrance to the tent of meeting and said, 'Our father died in the wilderness. He was not among Korah's followers, who banded together against the Lord, but he died for his own sin and left no sons. Why should our father's name disappear from his clan because he had no son? Give us property among our father's relatives.'"
—Numbers 27:2–4

Women tend to make less money than men, on average, and while that is a complex statistic with many contributing factors, one reason for this is that women are more likely to hesitate when it comes to asking for raises.

Zelophehad's daughters understood the power of asking. Even though it was a risk, they stepped forward, made their request, and laid out their reasoning. Moses inquired of God about their request, and not only did God say what they asked was right, he altered the law to make a path for daughters to inherit when a family had no sons. They were rewarded for their boldness, their humility, and their request to inherit.

We can find strength in these sisters' example. When we have a solid case and sound reasoning, we don't have to hesitate. And this certainly doesn't just apply to the workplace. It can apply to our personal lives and our lives at home or church. Whatever goals we're pursuing in our lives, let's be willing to ask!

Is there something you've been hoping for, but you haven't quite gotten up the courage to ask? As you journal about it, pray for God's wisdom—and the boldness to ask!

....

....

....

....

....

....

....

....

Rahab

> "The king of Jericho was told, 'Look, some of the
> Israelites have come here tonight to spy out the land.' So
> the king of Jericho sent this message to Rahab: 'Bring
> out the men who came to you and entered your house,
> because they have come to spy out the whole land.'"
> —Joshua 2:2–3

Rahab was not part of the Israelite community at first. She was a Canaanite, and the first time she's mentioned in the Bible, she's referred to as "a prostitute named Rahab" (Joshua 2:1). Not particularly flattering, and not the beginnings we'd expect from a hero of the faith like Rahab.

Why is she a hero? Rahab risked her safety, and possibly her life, to help the Hebrew strangers. It might make us think of Jesus' words in John 15:13: "Greater love has no one than this: to lay down one's life for one's friends." Those are words of intense bravery.

It runs against our natural instinct (self-preservation) to sacrifice ourselves for others. We may not ever experience a demand for self-sacrifice as dramatic as Rahab did here, although many in the 1940s were faced with a frighteningly similar situation as Jewish refugees fled from Nazis during World War II.

But self-sacrifice happens in quiet ways too. It happens in being an emotional support for a struggling friend, in taking care of our children day in and day out, in volunteering time, energy, and material resources to help those in need. It happens in putting others first and showing sacrificial love in moments small and large.

In the coming week, what are some ways you could show sacrificial love to those around you?

....

....

....

....

....

....

....

....

....

Aksah

"[Aksah] replied [to her father, Caleb], 'Do me
a special favor. Since you have given me land
in the Negev, give me also springs of water.' So
Caleb gave her the upper and lower springs.
—Joshua 15:19

The years of desert wandering were over. Joshua and Caleb
alone of Moses' generation led the people into the promised
land. Caleb offered his daughter Aksah in marriage to the man who
conquered Kiriath Sepher. She was off to marry the conquering
hero, Othniel, and that's when she made this request of her father.

Water was vital in the Negev desert. Because Aksah was specifically asking for springs, we might speculate the land Caleb offered
to her didn't have another water source. Whatever the original
water situation on the land, notice what her father did—he gave
her both the upper and lower springs.

Isn't that exactly like our heavenly father? In spite of all the
good things God has already given to us, when we come to him

with requests of necessity or deep desire, he hears us. And not only does he respond, he responds with something better than our original request.

That doesn't mean God gives us whatever we want, whenever we want it. Sometimes his response is a period of silence. Sometimes his response is a firm no. But God does always give us whatever is *best*, just like a loving father would. When we understand we have a loving father listening to our prayers, we can rest securely and peacefully in what he gives us. His choices are always wise.

Can you remember a time where God faithfully blessed you beyond what you even asked for? Or perhaps there's a desire deep in your heart you haven't given voice to yet. Ask your heavenly father now!

....

....

....

....

....

....

....

Deborah

"Now Deborah, a prophet, the wife of Lappidoth,
was leading Israel at that time. She held court under
the Palm of Deborah between Ramah and Bethel
in the hill country of Ephraim, and the Israelites
went up to her to have their disputes decided."
—Judges 4:4–5

You'd think that after the Israelites entered the promised land, everything would be peachy. But instead (because they were human), they entered into a cycle of falling away from God and his law, being handed over to their enemies, crying out to God, and God sending a deliverer to rescue and lead them. These deliverers were called judges, and Deborah was one of them.

Of the judges mentioned in the Bible, Deborah is the only woman. Was it hard for her to fit in among other Israelite women of her time? Maybe. They were running households and businesses, caring for livestock and fields—no small tasks—but Deborah was leading the nation.

Sometimes being the "only" of something feels like a negative thing. It can be lonely—the only woman powerlifting at the gym, the only single person at your women's Bible study, or the only Christian in the room. But being the "only" one means you're forging a path for others to follow in the future. "Only" means you're brave enough to do something outside the norm. Something others may be afraid to do or be or try. Like Deborah, your "only" can signal your strength.

Is there something you feel alone in right now? What are some ways God has used your "only" to bless you or perhaps encourage and inspire others?

Day 18

Jael

"But Jael, Heber's wife, picked up a tent peg and a hammer and went quietly to [Sisera] while he lay fast asleep, exhausted. She drove the peg through his temple into the ground, and he died."
—Judges 4:21

This is a shocking look into the story of our next biblical woman, Jael. Sisera was a commander of the army fighting the Israelites, who were under the leadership of Deborah. Sisera was trying to hide in the tent of a woman he wasn't related to—probably the last place anyone would think to look for him—and here Jael exacted the Lord's vengeance.

There's no getting around the violence of this act, but with this single act, Jael won Israel's war. While the gruesome nature of the killing might make us cringe, it's impossible to deny that Jael, who was certainly smaller, weaker, and more vulnerable than Sisera, the army commander, stepped up and slayed her giant. The Lord handed her victory, and she took it.

37

Each of us will face giants in our lives, figuratively speaking. Our giants are problems that seem impossible to solve. Goals that seem far out of reach. Persecution or hurtful behaviors of others. Our giants may even be in our own minds—fear, anxiety, depression, doubt.

Jael's story shows us that God's power is bigger than the biggest giants. Time and time again, the Bible shows us the weaker one overcoming the stronger, the smaller one overcoming the larger. Whatever giant you're facing today, God's got your back and then some.

What are some giants you're facing in your life right now? What are some giants God has helped you slay in the past?

....

....

....

....

....

....

....

....

Jephthah's Mother

"Jephthah the Gileadite was a mighty warrior. His father was Gilead; his mother was a prostitute."
—Judges 11:1

From Deborah to Jephthah, about a hundred years and four more judges passed. Obviously, Jephthah was a man, but his story starts here, with his unnamed mother. She gets this very unflattering one-liner as her primary mention in the Bible. We might wonder what single-sentence statement she would have written about herself, if given the opportunity. We might also wonder if she was able to raise her son, given that she was not married to his father. Did Jephthah stay in his father's household by himself instead? We just can't know for sure.

But Jephthah's less-than-ideal circumstances of birth—and the great role he would go on to have in Israel—tell us something important about God. There is no circumstance so shameful that

God can't redeem it. There is no person so weak that God can't work through her or him. There is no situation so hopeless that God can't restore balance.

In fact, God likes to do this. First Corinthians 1:27 says that God chose the weak to shame the strong. In other words, God's power is more clearly on display when he uses unlikely vessels to bring about his plans. Feeling like an unlikely vessel today? Be encouraged! God adores the "unlikely."

Shame is a powerful poison. Are there choices or circumstances of your past that seem to haunt you, never letting you forget, always making you doubt your place in God's family? Expel that poison!

....

....

....

....

....

....

....

Samson's Mother

"Then [Manoah's wife] went to her husband and told him, 'A man of God came to me. . . . he said to me, "You will become pregnant and have a son. Now then, drink no wine or other fermented drink and do not eat anything unclean, because the boy will be a Nazirite of God from the womb until the day of his death."'"
—Judges 13:6–7

Perhaps the most famous of all Israel's judges is Samson. His story in Scripture begins with his parents, Manoah and his unnamed wife, who had been unable to have children before an angel of the Lord came to her and told her she would have a son.

After the angel visited her, Samson's mother went straight to her husband to fill him in on the situation. She relayed the angel's message, repeating the wild, wonderful prophecy she'd just heard. Both of Samson's parents believed the angel's words.

Testimony is vital. "Testimony" is just another way to say "our stories" or "what we have witnessed." How many of us believe in Jesus Christ because someone else told us about him? Unless we've had an angelic visitation like Samson's mom, all of us probably heard about Jesus from another person. We heard their testimonies—their stories about what they had experienced and knew to be true—and faith was sparked in our hearts. We heard, and we believed.

Like Samson's mom, and like those who first shared their stories of Jesus with us, let's aim to have our powerful words of testimony reach others. Tell about the times God answered prayers for you. Share about how Jesus has changed your heart. You'll be planting faith-seeds in the hearts of your listeners.

Has anyone shared testimony with you that has been particularly powerful? What are some of the most powerful testimonies you could share from your own life?

Delilah

> "Then Delilah said to Samson, 'You have
> made a fool of me; you lied to me. Come
> now, tell me how you can be tied.'"
> —Judges 16:10

From what we know of Samson's parents, they seem pretty great. They tried to raise their son as instructed. But Samson had a hard time staying on course. He repeatedly went astray with Philistine women, most famously Delilah.

The Philistines offered Delilah a huge sum of money if she would get Samson to tell her the secret of his supernatural strength. Samson had fooled her once, and in Judges 16:10, we see her response to his trick.

Delilah's response to this situation was so audacious, it's almost funny (except it's not). She had just betrayed her man to his enemies, and when she discovered he lied about the proper way to subdue him, she pouted. How dare Samson refuse to tell her the best way to capture and kill him? Wow.

While we might not be as disrespectful as Delilah was, everyone is vulnerable to a similar temptation—emotional manipulation. Delilah tried to guilt-trip Samson. She tried to make him feel bad for making her look foolish. Have you ever tried something similar? Maybe tried to make someone feel bad so they'd give you something you want?

It's important we avoid emotional manipulation in all its forms, whether a small guilt trip or a brazen pout session. When we have ulterior motives lurking beneath our words, we chip away at the trust others have in us. Honest and straightforward is always best!

What are some qualities you can nurture in yourself to encourage straightforward communication—for example, focusing on the truth or paying close attention to others' feelings?

....

....

....

....

....

....

....

Naomi & Orpah

> "'May the Lord grant that each of you will find rest in the
> home of another husband.' Then [Naomi] kissed [her daughters-
> in-law, Orpah and Ruth] goodbye and they wept aloud and
> said to her, 'We will go back with you to your people.'"
> —Ruth 1:9–10

Because of a famine in the land of Judah, Naomi, her husband, and her two sons traveled to Moab. There Naomi's husband died; her sons married Moabite women, Orpah and Ruth; and then both sons died, leaving the three women alone. Naomi decided to return to Judah and encouraged her daughters-in-law to return to their people and find new husbands so they would be supported. That brings us to this verse.

This is such an awesome display of affection between Naomi and her daughters-in-law. Our culture likes to stereotype a lot of relationships as being difficult or negative—parent/child, teacher/student, boss/employee, and maybe most of all, in-laws. But it doesn't have to be that way!

Some relationships are difficult, and some *people* are difficult, but sometimes we enter into a situation expecting it to be bad before anything bad has actually happened. Naomi and her daughters-in-law, who clearly adored her, defy the in-law stereotype. It's wise for us to enter into new relationships and situations with the belief that this kind of harmony is possible. Then, as far as it depends upon us, we can contribute toward making that possibility a reality.

We can't control others' behavior, but we can always control our own mindset and endeavor to bring peace, blessing, and unity to our relationships.

Is there a relationship or situation in your life that you haven't given a fair chance yet? What are some ways you can make some changes or orchestrate a fresh start?

Ruth

"But Ruth replied, 'Don't urge me to leave you or to turn back from you. Where you go I will go, and where you stay I will stay. Your people will be my people and your God my God. Where you die I will die, and there I will be buried. May the LORD deal with me, be it ever so severely, if even death separates you and me.'"
—Ruth 1:16–17

This, perhaps more than any other passage, reveals Ruth's heart. Orpah left and returned home, as Naomi urged her— and that wasn't particularly wrong. But when we contrast Ruth's choice with Orpah's, we see how deeply committed Ruth was to Naomi and Naomi's God. She was so committed she was willing to give up her homeland and people. Ruth knew she had found something better than what she was born into.

Some people may seem like they have been blessed with absolutely everything: the perfect family, an excellent career, a comfortable financial situation. . . . But the truth is, no matter how outwardly perfect anyone's life looks (and we better remind ourselves that everyone has troubles to deal with in their lives), we are all designed for something "better than our birth."

And that's because the world we're all born into is marred by sin. Our world is warped because sin has entered it. It's not as God originally designed. So, deep down in all our hearts, we're longing for something better—that sinless world, which will return when Jesus does. How cool is that? We were designed for something greater!

Is there a time in your life when you left the comfort and safety of your "norm"? How was God faithful to you in that situation?

....

....

....

....

....

....

....

....

....

Hannah & Peninnah

"[Elkanah] had two wives; one was called
Hannah and the other Peninnah. Peninnah
had children, but Hannah had none."
—1 Samuel 1:2

This short verse gives us a sad, succinct introduction to
Hannah. Her husband had two wives, and Hannah was "the
one with none." We can guess that a situation like this—one man,
two wives—would usually lead to a fair amount of rivalry at the
best of times. But when one woman was able to have children and
the other wasn't, it had to have been drastically worse. Remember
Rachel and Leah . . .

Dealing with rivalry isn't easy, especially when you're "the one
with none." Maybe you grew up feeling competitive with a sibling, and that sibling excels at something you don't. Maybe that
carried over into your adult life, and you find yourself comparing

with friends, colleagues, or even that sibling still. Sometimes we gain what feels like a victory and become "the one with some," but those victories are fleeting. If we're chasing those, we'll never be completely satisfied.

The long-term solution is to understand that we aren't created for comparison. You were created with unique gifts to use, particular trials to overcome, and specific triumphs to celebrate. When you embrace your own path and avoid falling into the comparison trap, you can find contentment, as well as the motivation to be the very best *you* possible.

Have you struggled with competition and comparison that leaves you feeling empty? Write out some of the wonderful, unique qualities God has blessed you with—he made you *you* on purpose!

Michal

> "When David returned home to bless his household,
> Michal daughter of Saul came out to meet him and
> said, 'How the king of Israel has distinguished himself
> today, going around half-naked in full view of the slave
> girls of his servants as any vulgar fellow would!'"
> —2 Samuel 6:20

We've reached the era of kings with this story of Israel's most famous king, David, and his wife Michal. Sadly, this exchange between David and Michal is what she's most remembered for, but their story began with love (1 Samuel 18:20–29), and Michal had even saved David's life from her father, Saul (1 Samuel 19:11).

Michal was embarrassed by how David was behaving in front of the entire city—and nation. Hey, it's possible David was being improper. It's possible those slave girls were seeing a bit more of their king than they needed to (just sayin' . . .). But Michal let her visceral reaction to her husband's outward behavior override her ability to see his worshipful heart.

It's shockingly easy to care more about the outside than the inside. Maybe you've felt awkward attending a church event because your wardrobe feels inferior to everyone else's. Or maybe you've shied away from serving in the choir or worship team because, even though God's given you the heart for it, you worry about standing in front of all those people. Remember that God cares about your worshipful heart, not your outward appearance. He cares about your love for him, not how polished you are. Let's try to have David's attitude, not Michal's.

Has worrying about outward appearances ever stopped you from serving in a way God has pressed on your heart? What are some ways you can combat those fears and focus on the heart?

....

....

....

....

....

....

....

....

Abigail

"[David said the LORD] 'has kept his servant from
doing wrong and has brought Nabal's wrongdoing
down on his own head.' Then David sent word to
Abigail, asking her to become his wife. His servants
went to Carmel and said to Abigail, 'David has sent
us to you to take you to become his wife.'"
—1 Samuel 25:39–40

This must have been quite a surprise for Abigail. When she
and David last parted ways, she was returning home to her
foolish, wicked husband, Nabal. Abigail had just ensured Nabal's
safety after he'd caused offense to David, who was the anointed
future king at this time. Abigail acted swiftly and wisely, showing respect and deference to David, hoping to save the lives of her
household. We can imagine she had no idea that a few weeks later,
Nabal would be dead by God's hand and David would be asking
her to become his wife.

Sometimes we think we have the "best-case scenario" all figured out. We think we know the most wonderful thing that could possibly happen. Abigail probably thought soothing David's anger and undoing Nabal's mess was the best thing that could happen. And then God surprised her with an unexpected blessing—David as her husband instead.

What's the last "best-case scenario" you asked God for? Imagine for a second that he gave you that, plus something wildly better. It doesn't always work this way, of course. God always gives us what we *need*, and sometimes that's the bare minimum. But sometimes it's a whole lot more!

What is the most pressing need in your life right now? Whether God responds with the bare minimum or much, much more, you can rest assured that his answer is always the best answer.

Bathsheba

"[Bathsheba] conceived and sent word to
David, saying, 'I am pregnant.'"
—2 Samuel 11:5

We can suppose this was a moment of pure panic for both Bathsheba and David. David had committed adultery with the wife of one of his warriors, Uriah, while Uriah was away fighting wars. Now what were they supposed to do? The sin of adultery is a huge deal, and Bathsheba's pregnancy certainly threatened to make the king's sin very public, very soon.

While being very careful not to excuse David's behavior—because frankly, there's nothing okay about what he did—we can probably all agree that everyone makes mistakes. Not just little mistakes, but huge, massive blunders. We've each probably had a handful of our own, so we can likely relate to the fear and shame David and Bathsheba may have felt.

So what do we do when we realize we've stumbled big-time? The very thing we fear most—confess it. That seems like a crazy idea when you're caught in a fear-and-shame tornado. But honestly confessing to someone you trust helps pull you *out* of that downward spiral. It stops the bleeding and helps begin the process of repentance and healing. It's scary, for sure, but it's healthy—and necessary!

Have you ever been caught in a fear-and-shame spiral in the wake of a difficult situation? Maybe you're there now. Start with confession to the Lord, then think about a highly trusted friend you can talk to.

Tamar

"Then Amnon said to Tamar, 'Bring the food here into my bedroom so I may eat from your hand.' And Tamar took the bread she had prepared and brought it to her brother Amnon in his bedroom. But when she took it to him to eat, he grabbed her and said, 'Come to bed with me, my sister.'"
—2 Samuel 13:10–11

Tamar's story is devastating. Sadly, sexual abuse continues to be pervasive. "One out of every five American women has been the victim of an attempted or completed rape."[1] Sexual abuse occurs in schools, workplaces, and even churches. It occurs within families. Tamar's story is devastating, but this topic is important. Her story is our story.

Tamar was trying to obey her father, King David, and serve her brother. She was trying to do the right thing. What happened to her was in no way the result of her desires or her choices. How can that be? How can our good intentions go so horribly wrong?

There's no satisfying answer to this, except to understand that we live in a broken world, marred by sin and distorted from what God originally intended. We can do everything "right" and still people may try to hurt us. Not only try, but succeed. Understand, beloved daughter of God, that this is not what God would wish for us. This is a result of mankind's brokenness.

We can take steps to protect ourselves. We can learn self-defense techniques to help us escape if we're physically threatened. We can trust our instincts. When something feels "off," it's okay to get out of that situation, even if you think you might be overreacting. We can look out for warning signs and learn to identify manipulative behavior. We can take precautions to help keep ourselves safe. But please know that the failures of these safety measures *do not* make abuse your fault.

Tamar's full story can be read in 2 Samuel 13, including Amnon's response after he assaults Tamar. What does his behavior illustrate about sin? Do you find anything about Tamar's story particularly surprising?

Queen of Sheba

"When the queen of Sheba heard about the fame of Solomon and his relationship to the LORD, she came to test Solomon with hard questions. Arriving at Jerusalem with a very great caravan—with camels carrying spices, large quantities of gold, and precious stones—she came to Solomon and talked with him about all that she had on her mind."
—1 Kings 10:1–2

David's throne eventually passed to his son Solomon. Solomon is remembered as the wisest man who ever lived. His knowledge was something to behold. It was so legendary, the queen of Sheba traveled from southwestern Arabia (in present-day Yemen) to pick his brain.

The queen is another fascinating non-Israelite woman who, on some level, recognized God's special relationship with Israel. She came for Solomon's wisdom but also because she'd heard about his relationship with the Lord. Jesus spoke of the queen of Sheba. In Matthew 12:42 he said: "The Queen of the South will rise at the judgment with this generation and condemn it; for she came from the ends of the earth to listen to Solomon's wisdom, and now something greater than Solomon is here." She is an example of someone who doesn't yet have a relationship with God but may be seeking him.

Even today in our modern society, women are sometimes told they shouldn't seek education. Some are even told they shouldn't seek knowledge. But the Bible doesn't condemn the queen of Sheba for her curiosity. It doesn't deride her thirst for knowledge or her quest for wisdom. Nor did Solomon, it seems, because he answered all her questions. What an amazing opportunity he had to share about the Lord!

Do you have any seekers in your life—those who aren't churchgoers but who seem curious about God? What can you do to nurture those relationships?

....

....

....

....

....

....

....

Jezebel

"So Ahab went home, sullen and angry because
Naboth the Jezreelite had said, 'I will not give you the
inheritance of my ancestors.' He lay on his bed sulking
and refused to eat.... Jezebel his wife said, 'Is this how
you act as king over Israel? Get up and eat! Cheer up.
I'll get you the vineyard of Naboth the Jezreelite.'"
—1 Kings 21:4.7

We have looked at many fantastic biblical women who are
role models. Needless to say, Queen Jezebel isn't one of
them. She's often portrayed as being sexually immoral, but her primary sin was actually idolatry. Jezebel was deeply religious. She just happened to worship Baal and other false gods.

In a different context, Jezebel's words here might be positive
and encouraging. *Get up! Cheer up! You're the king! No pouting.* But
in this context, her words are terrifying. She said that as king over
Israel, nothing was off-limits for Ahab. He should have cheered
up, looked alive, because no matter what Naboth said, Jezebel was

going to get that vineyard for her husband. In fact, she was about to orchestrate Naboth's murder. Yikes.

It's important that we make sure our positions of power or privilege don't go to our heads. It's easy to lose perspective and get full of ourselves when we're given power. But that's such a dangerous place to be! It can lead to bad decisions that hurt other people. Ahab and Jezebel are extreme examples, but it's easy to fall into the same trap in smaller ways if we're not careful.

Let's take a moment to pray for humble hearts and the desire to serve others, especially when we're put in leadership positions. With the right focus, we can be effective, godly leaders.

Is there a time in your life where you've let power go to your head? What are some practices you can put into place to help you keep an eternal perspective as you lead others?

The Widow at Zarephath

"Elijah said to [the widow], 'Don't be afraid. Go home
and do as you have said. But first make a small loaf of
bread for me from what you have and bring it to me,
and then make something for yourself and your son. For
this is what the LORD, the God of Israel, says: "The jar of
flour will not be used up and the jug of oil will not run
dry until the day the LORD sends rain on the land.""'
—1 Kings 17:13–14

The great prophet Elijah had been sent outside Israel and
Judah to the land where Jezebel's father was king. (Yikes.)
The Lord led him to this widow, specifically. As we read Elijah's
request of the widow here, it's important to remember two things.
First, Elijah was in a pagan land. This was not a people group who
had a relationship with God. Second, the widow was literally about
to starve—she'd just told Elijah so (1 Kings 17:12).

Essentially, Elijah was asking her to give *everything* she had to a God she probably didn't know.

As we continue the story, we learn that the widow "did as Elijah had told her," and the Lord performed a miracle of provision for her (1 Kings 17:15–16). She and her son did not starve to death, after all.

Take a second to think about what it might mean if God asked you to trust in him so completely, you had to give *all*, whether that was everything you owned or maybe simply the one thing most important to you. Could you do it? Would you be willing?

Those are tough questions. Jesus made similar requests in the New Testament (Matthew 8:21–22; Matthew 19:16–30; Mark 8:34). If you feel like your own response to Jesus' call is lacking the zeal you want, you can pray for the Holy Spirit to help you grow in willingness to surrender to God's perfect will in your life.

If you were asked to give "your all" to follow God, what would that mean for you? Are there some things you would not be willing to give up?

....

....

....

....

....

....

The Widow of a Prophet

"The wife of a man from the company of the prophets cried out to Elisha, 'Your servant my husband is dead, and you know that he revered the LORD. But now his creditor is coming to take my two boys as his slaves.'"

—2 Kings 4:1

Here we have another unnamed woman, known simply as "the widow of a prophet" to us. You may have noticed we're now dealing with Elisha the prophet instead of Elijah. Elijah mentored young Elisha, and Elisha took over his ministry after Elijah ascended to heaven. Elisha may not be as famous, but he performed twice the number of miracles as his mentor.

Maybe that's why the prophet's widow came to this man of God. She was totally desperate, and she needed help from someone trustworthy. King Jehoram, Ahab and Jezebel's son, was on the throne. He encouraged Baal worship like his mother had. The prophet's wife would have been in a precarious situation even with her husband alive, but now that he was dead, she was facing total destitution and the loss of her remaining family. But she was not ashamed to cry out to God and God's representative, the prophet Elisha.

It's okay to ask for help when we feel overwhelmed. It's okay to cry out when we're afraid. It doesn't mean we don't have faith. In fact, it means the opposite. When we're facing an overwhelming situation, crying out for help shows that we believe in God's ability to answer those cries!

Do you have a hard time asking for help when you need it? Think about why this may be (self-reliance, fear of judgment, or something else entirely), and brainstorm some ways to disrupt those thought patterns.

The Shunamite Woman

"One day Elisha went to Shunem. And a well-to-do woman was there, who urged him to stay for a meal. So whenever he came by, he stopped there to eat. She said to her husband, 'I know that this man who often comes our way is a holy man of God. Let's make a small room on the roof and put in it a bed and a table, a chair and a lamp for him. Then he can stay there whenever he comes to us.'"
—2 Kings 4:8–10

We don't know her name, but this exceptional woman of the Bible is sometimes called "the Shunamite woman who was hospitable to Elisha." Providing hospitality and contributing to the needs of those in the church, especially those in ministry, is something Paul encouraged the early church to do (Romans 12:13). We show hospitality to others because it's an outward expression of God's care and grace. Hospitality and caring for the needs of others reflect God's heart of love, compassion, and self-sacrifice.

The Shunamite woman's hospitality would be admirable under any circumstances, but it's especially cool when you consider her whole backstory (2 Kings 4:13–16). She had material wealth, but she'd never had children. Not only was being a mother important in her culture, it seems to have been personally important to her.

But being childless didn't stop her from blessing others. Sometimes it's hard to be generous when we don't have everything we want in life. Maybe we fixate on our own desires rather than focusing on others' needs. Maybe we feel angry, hurt, or bitter that God hasn't responded to our requests the way we hoped.

The Shunamite woman is a great example to help us combat those attitudes! She gave without expectation or ulterior motive. She gave even though she still had unfulfilled desires of her own.

What are some ways you can cultivate hospitality and generosity in your life? Do these traits come easily to you, or is this something that's a little more challenging?

Athaliah

"When Athaliah the mother of Ahaziah
saw that her son was dead, she proceeded
to destroy the whole royal family."
—2 Kings 11:1

Athaliah was a relative by marriage to Ahab and Jezebel's house. She followed in their footsteps of evil, as did her son, the king, and it wasn't pretty (2 Kings 8:26–27). At the root of Jezebel's wickedness was her deeply religious idolatry. At the root of Athaliah's wickedness was her thirst for power. Her son had been king, but when he died, she decided she ought to become queen regnant. In order for that to happen, all the heirs to the throne had to be destroyed. So she killed the remnant of her own dynasty, including her grandsons, making sure no one stood in her way.

Athaliah was a brutally wicked woman. But the desire for power can even cause otherwise decent people to do some terrible things. Ever watched the way many candidates behave during important elections? Or seen news headlines about businesspeople caught in illegal activity as they sought to build their powerful, successful business? Or those whose empires are built on the backs of severely underpaid laborers?

Power itself isn't evil. And the drive to be successful isn't bad. But when the thirst for power drowns out all else and makes your moral center wobbly, it's time to reevaluate. Being a godly woman who has ambition means behaving ethically while working hard for your dreams. Don't let your drive make you forget who God created you to be!

Would you describe yourself as ambitious—someone with big dreams and the drive to get you to those goals? Write down some nonnegotiable virtues you will bring with you as you pursue your passions.

....

....

....

....

....

....

....

Jehosheba

"But Jehosheba, the daughter of King Jehoram and sister of Ahaziah, took Joash son of Ahaziah and stole him away from among the royal princes, who were about to be murdered. She put him and his nurse in a bedroom to hide him from Athaliah; so he was not killed. He remained hidden with his nurse at the temple of the LORD for six years while Athaliah ruled the land."
—2 Kings 11:2–3

Mercifully, we have a bright light in the midst of Athaliah's dark time. Her name was Jehosheba, and she shows us how compassion and love are great strengths. Jehosheba was the daughter of Athaliah's husband, though she may have had a different mother. Joash, Athaliah's grandson, was Jehosheba's nephew. Confused yet? The main thing to understand is that Jehosheba defied a powerful family member to save a very vulnerable one—Joash.

Jehosheba shows us how risky, powerful, and strong love can be. If Athaliah had discovered what Jehosheba had done, Jehosheba would have likely been executed. But Jehosheba was willing to risk it all to save her nephew's life.

Sometimes, facing the evil and suffering of this world can be overwhelming. Where do we even begin to help when there's so much to do? We can follow Jehosheba's example and pick *one thing*—one person, one cause, one ministry, and start there. We might not be able to change the world overnight. But we can change one person's world. We can help shape one community. We can pour our whole hearts into one special cause. You'd be surprised how great an impact you can have when you focus your efforts!

If you were to pick your "one" right now, what would it be? Is there a specific person on your heart to mentor or a cause you're passionate about? Consider where you might focus your impact on this world.

....

....

....

....

....

....

....

Sheerah

"His daughter was Sheerah, who built Lower and
Upper Beth Horon as well as Uzzen Sheerah."
—1 Chronicles 7:24

Did you know there is a person named Sheerah mentioned in the Bible? It wouldn't be surprising if you didn't. She's only mentioned in this one verse! But it's a pretty cool verse, isn't it? She was Sheerah, the city-builder.

We know female city-builders weren't the norm in Sheerah's day, which is why she is so notable. But this one verse about her shows us that throughout history, women have been defying expectations. We don't know what else is true of Sheerah, since we only get this one snippet about her. She may have also been a wife, mother, and homemaker, like many of the women of her day. Or she may have only been a builder. But, either way, she was definitely a bit outside the norm!

It's important that we do the work God has equipped us for, not necessarily what our culture expects of us. Culture shifts.

Expectations change. But God doesn't. When he gifts you for a certain kind of work or calls you to a certain thing, following through on that gifting or calling is always the right choice. Have you ever defied the norm? You're in good company!

What are some outside-the-norm things God has called you to do in your life?

....

....

....

....

....

....

....

....

....

....

Huldah

> "Hilkiah and those the king had sent with him went to
> speak to the prophet Huldah, who was the wife of Shallum
> son of Tokhath, the son of Hasrah, keeper of the wardrobe.
> She lived in Jerusalem, in the New Quarter. She said to
> them, 'This is what the Lord, the God of Israel, says.'"
> —2 Chronicles 34:22–23

We've already seen female prophets Miriam and Deborah, and now we meet Huldah. There are plenty of examples of women of God who are explicitly described as being prophets. Some were married, like Huldah and Deborah. Another was a widow (Anna, who we'll meet later). And some, like Philip's daughters, were young, unmarried women.

Whatever else God calls you to in your life—marriage, motherhood, career—you are not disqualified from ministry. God can and will use you, if you're willing. We're not all prophets, but we are all useful.

Huldah spoke the very words of God directly to the people,

just like a male prophet. Too often, we discount ourselves from powerful ministry like this. Denominations vary as to what level of leadership women are allowed to hold, but even if you are a member of a denomination that doesn't allow women into leadership roles, you can still *minister* in powerful ways.

Sometimes we think the word *ministry* means *pastoring*. And that is one way it can be used. But teachers also minister. Mentors minister. Those who serve behind the scenes minister. Those who speak the good news of the gospel minister, even though they're not speaking from behind a pulpit. God has prepared ministry opportunities for *you*, using your talents and gifts. Will you take him up on that offer?

What are some of your gifts God has used in the past for ministry? What are some he hasn't yet tapped into but one day may?

....

....

....

....

....

....

....

Queen Vashti

"Therefore, if it pleases the king, let him issue a royal decree and let it be written in the laws of Persia and Media, which cannot be repealed, that Vashti is never again to enter the presence of King Xerxes. Also let the king give her royal position to someone else who is better than she."
—Esther 1:19

O uch. Deposed from her position as queen? Banished from the king's presence forever? And the final parting shot—they will start looking for a queen who is "better than she." Double ouch.

And all because Vashti refused to obey a demeaning command put forth by her husband, Xerxes, as he partied with his noblemen. The cultural context is important to understand. This Persian queen would have generally lived in seclusion, so this was not a simple request her husband made. He asked her to submit to objectification, and she said no. She chose what was right and was utterly rejected for it.

We can hope she had supporters around her who let her know

she was loved and valued by them, even if Xerxes had cast her aside. Sadly, as a Persian queen, she probably didn't know the God of the Jewish people. And that's a shame. Because when all our earthly relationships fail, when we feel rejected by everyone on Earth, God is *always* there.

God's presence in our lives doesn't depend on how awesome we feel from one day to the next. His presence is guaranteed, no matter what. He has deemed us worthy and accepted through the blood of Jesus. There is no surer, stronger foundation upon which to rest when we feel rejected by others.

Have you ever felt the sharp slap of rejection? How did you handle it, and what are some ways you might handle it in the future?

Esther

> "Then Esther sent this reply to Mordecai: 'Go, gather together all the Jews who are in Susa, and fast for me. Do not eat or drink for three days, night or day. I and my attendants will fast as you do. When this is done, I will go to the king, even though it is against the law. And if I perish, I perish.'"
> —Esther 4:15–16

The woman ultimately chosen to replace deposed Queen Vashti was Esther, a Jewish exile living in Persia with her uncle Mordecai. The Jews faced genocide, and Mordecai challenged his niece to step up for her people and approach the king, even though doing so would risk her life.

If Mordecai's challenge was a powerful one, then Esther's faithful response was every bit as powerful. Despite her initial reluctance, Esther strapped on her (figurative) sword and got ready for battle.

Mordecai sensed that Esther had the chance to be part of God's big-picture plan here—and he was right! But Esther had a choice in this moment. She could have backed away and hoped for her own safety and deliverance for her people from some other source. Or she had the opportunity to take a risk, respond in faith, and be part of the plan.

"God moments" happen in our lives, too—those crazy "coincidences" where we're in the perfect place at the perfect time. But, like Esther, we have to respond to those moments. Let's pray God will open our eyes—and our hearts—to better see those times when he wants us to be part of his big-picture plan.

Can you think of a time when you felt you were born "for such a time as this" (Esther 4:14)?

....

....

....

....

....

....

....

....

....

Elizabeth

"After this his wife Elizabeth became pregnant
and for five months remained in seclusion.
'The Lord has done this for me,' she said. 'In
these days he has shown his favor and taken
away my disgrace among the people.'"
—Luke 1:24–25

We've made it to the New Testament! Elizabeth's story starts
out in a tough place. She and her husband did an excellent
job following the law of Moses as best they could. They are called
"blameless," and still she could not conceive a child. But then one
day an angel declared Elizabeth's world was about to change—she
would have a son and name him John, and John would help bring
people back to the Lord (Luke 1:5–16).

Can you imagine what it was like to be in Elizabeth's shoes?
She went from an elderly, barren woman who considered herself
"disgraced" among the people to the mother of a miracle child. Just
like that, her entire identity changed.

God is in the habit of doing that. Our relationship with Jesus brings us from darkness to light. We were blind; now we see. We were dead in our sins; now we live. Believing in Jesus changes our identity in these ways and others.

That's a pretty deep thought! But the apostle Paul wrote about it a lot—becoming a new person in Christ. When you're struggling with something—anything from a bad habit to a devastating season of life—you can find hope, strength, and encouragement in this fact. You are a new creature in Jesus, with a totally new identity as God's beloved daughter.

What are some new bits of identity being a follower of Christ has given to you? A compassionate heart, a thirst for the truth, a hospitable home, or something else entirely?

Mary, Mother of Jesus

"In the sixth month of Elizabeth's pregnancy, God sent the angel Gabriel to Nazareth, a town in Galilee, to a virgin pledged to be married to a man named Joseph, a descendant of David. The virgin's name was Mary. The angel went to her and said, 'Greetings, you who are highly favored! The Lord is with you.'"
—Luke 1:26–28

We've reached the most famous woman in the Bible— actually, one of the most famous women in all history! Mary, the mother of Jesus. For two thousand years, people have been reading about, writing about, and painting portraits of Mary. By most accounts, she was simply a young woman. She wasn't a princess or a prophet or a military leader. She was just a normal girl.

Isn't it cool to think about how much God entrusted to this regular girl? He judged her capable of shouldering this sizable burden—and honor. She wasn't disqualified because she was young or because she was "normal." God looked at her heart and said, "Yes. You're the one."

We, as humans, tend to like superheroes. Our culture glorifies those who are talented and beautiful, wealthy and powerful. But God chose a normal girl with superhero-strength faith. When the angel declared the miracle to come—a virgin birth—Mary didn't doubt, scoff, or laugh. She said, "May your word to me be fulfilled" (Luke 1:38).

This is what God asks of us. We don't need to be rich in the currency of the world—simply filled with the kind of faith that says, "Yes, God. May your will come to pass—I'm here to help."

If you were in Mary's shoes—keeping in mind she was probably around twelve to fourteen years old—how do you think you would have responded? What are ways you might infuse some Mary-sized faith in your life?

Anna

"There was also a prophet, Anna, the daughter of Penuel, of the tribe of Asher. She was very old; she had lived with her husband seven years after her marriage, and then was a widow until she was eighty-four. She never left the temple but worshiped night and day, fasting and praying."
—Luke 2:36–37

Another female prophet! Anna doesn't have a ton of space devoted to her story, but she was a pretty cool lady. She was married for a relatively short time, then her husband died. She lived the rest of her life as a widow and devoted most—maybe all—of her time to worshiping God. Wow!

Anna is a great encouragement for those who feel called to devote their lives to God's service instead of marriage and family. But even those of us who are married and have children (or would like those things someday) can adopt a little bit of Anna's spirit.

Anna was a true prophet, and she was bold about it. When she saw Jesus' family enter the temple, she "[came] up to them at that very moment . . . gave thanks to God and spoke about the child to all who were looking forward to the redemption of Jerusalem" (Luke 2:38).

How can you be bold for the kingdom this week? Maybe it means ministering to that friend who has been asking about God lately. Or maybe it means simply showing the love of Jesus by helping someone through a tough time. Wherever the need, you can draw inspiration from Anna by serving with your whole heart and with a constant focus on your love for God.

Brainstorm three specific ways you can show your love of God to others this week. Then select your favorite one and take action!

The Samaritan Woman at the Well

"The Samaritan woman said to him, 'You are a Jew and I am a Samaritan woman. How can you ask me for a drink?' (For Jews do not associate with Samaritans.) Jesus answered her, 'If you knew the gift of God and who it is that asks you for a drink, you would have asked him and he would have given you living water.'"
—John 4:9–10

There was a lot that could have potentially separated Jesus from the woman at the well. The fact that she was a woman, for one—Jesus and this woman were not considered social equals in biblical times. And there's obviously the fact that she was a Samaritan. Jesus could have turned away, ignored the woman, or even been rude to her—that's what his culture would have expected.

We find out later in their conversation that this woman was also living in sin with a man she was not married to. Jesus could have turned away from her on that basis, too.

But even early in his ministry, Jesus was seen breaking through all those barriers to reach out to this woman drawing water.

There is nothing that disqualifies us from receiving God's grace. There is no sin in your past—no boundaries of culture, ethnicity, or gender—that separate you from redemption, if you have faith. It's hard for us to believe that sometimes, but it's true. It's the foundation of Jesus' work on earth—to bring *all mankind* back to his father. No one is left out. The offer of salvation is for all. And stories like that of the Samaritan woman at the well show us God's heart in this.

Have you ever worried there are barriers between you and the love of God? Maybe you felt that way before you knew Jesus, but how has your understanding changed now?

....

....

....

....

....

....

Herodias & Salome

"On Herod's birthday the daughter of Herodias danced
for the guests and pleased Herod so much that he
promised with an oath to give her whatever she
asked. Prompted by her mother, she said, 'Give me
here on a platter the head of John the Baptist.'"
—Matthew 14:6–8

Herodias held quite the grudge against John the Baptist
because he dared to point out her sinful relationship with
Herod (Mark 6:17–20). Traditionally, Herodias's daughter was
known as Salome, even though we don't see her name mentioned in
the Bible. And boy, did she follow in her mom's malicious footsteps.
This coldhearted request was prompted by Herodias's grudge—but
also by John's message. Herodias wanted John's message of repentance silenced, and these were the drastic measures she and Salome
took to make that happen.

It's hard to tell how much of this wicked deed was Salome's
doing and how much was Herodias's. Matthew 14:8 says, "prompted

by her mother." Does that mean Salome wouldn't have done this if not for her mom's nudging? Did she feel pressured or forced? Or was she totally on board, eager to make it happen?

It is unfortunately common to find ourselves in situations where we're being nudged to do things we're not comfortable with. Sometimes it helps us stand firm when we remember God's opinion is the one that should matter most to us. It's natural to care what other people think. But we need to allow God the final say in our lives. When someone is pressuring you to do something that feels wrong, stand firm! God will strengthen your resolve, if you ask him.

Have you been in a situation where you felt nudged in a direction you didn't want to go? What are some strategies to employ in these moments?

....

....

....

....

....

....

The Sinful Woman

"A woman in that town who lived a sinful life learned that Jesus was eating at the Pharisee's house, so she came there with an alabaster jar of perfume. As she stood behind him at his feet weeping, she began to wet his feet with her tears. Then she wiped them with her hair, kissed them and poured perfume on them."
—Luke 7:37–38

Heartbrokenness. It's the only word to describe this woman's attitude as she approached Jesus. We might wonder what her background was. How did she hear about Jesus? How did she know to come to him for the wholeness she sought? What had she done in her life that branded her as a sinner in the eyes of those surrounding Jesus?

We don't have the answers to these questions. But we do see something so touching, so beautiful, from our Savior in this moment. This story shows us that our pasts are irrelevant. The love of Jesus finds us wherever we are, even when we've made mistakes.

Maybe you have some dark mistakes in your past. If so, you're not alone. People with dark pasts have been coming to Jesus for millennia. He doesn't reject those seeking to turn their lives around.

Maybe that message is for you to receive today. Maybe you need to be reminded of the deep forgiveness and love Jesus offers to each of us. But this message is also for all of us as we grow in Christlikeness, seeking to echo Jesus' actions in our own lives. Our savior modeled gentleness and compassion to a broken woman who believed. Let's follow his lead!

Jesus declared this woman's sins forgiven (Luke 7:47). How can you walk in confidence today, knowing your sins, too, are forgiven?

....

....

....

....

....

....

....

....

The Woman Subject to Bleeding

"Immediately her bleeding stopped and she felt in her body that she was freed from her suffering. . . . Then the woman, knowing what had happened to her, came and fell at [Jesus'] feet and, trembling with fear, told him the whole truth. He said to her, 'Daughter, your faith has healed you. Go in peace and be freed from your suffering.'"
- Mark 5:29, 33–34

Ah, this is beautiful. This woman had been bleeding for twelve years. She had tried everything, spent all she had on doctors, but nothing worked. Even so, she came to Jesus, secretly believing if she could just touch him, she would be healed.

The sick woman's faith that Jesus' touch would heal translated into actual healing for her. After all those years of suffering, her body was whole! Hallelujah!

But we have to be really careful with this. We must both affirm that God absolutely can and does heal (because he still does perform miracles like this!), but we must also acknowledge that even those with faith as deep and true as this sick woman's can suffer illness. Sometimes for their whole lives. Sometimes they even die. We have to be careful that we do not equate their suffering—or *our* suffering—with a lack of faith. Paul mentioned the "thorn in [his] flesh" that God would not take away in 2 Corinthians 12:7. Job suffered many physical trials, even though it had nothing to do with his faith or lack thereof. Sometimes God allows suffering, and we don't always get to know why. That's a difficult truth but an important one to acknowledge.

Have you ever suffered with something—whether physically, spiritually, or emotionally—that God chose not to take away or heal instantaneously? Did you find your faith strengthened through that trial?

....

....

....

....

....

....

....

The Woman Caught in Adultery

"But Jesus bent down and started to write on the
ground with his finger. When they kept on questioning
him, he straightened up and said to them, 'Let any
one of you who is without sin be the first to throw a
stone at her.' Again he stooped down and wrote on
the ground. At this, those who heard began to go away
one at a time, the older ones first, until only Jesus
was left, with the woman still standing there."
—John 8:6–9

This is such a beautiful picture of the heart of Jesus. He knew
what was in the minds of the Pharisees. He knew they were
seeking to trap him and not at all concerned about this woman
or her relationship with God (John 8:6). His heart was to redeem
this woman—to save her and not condemn her. Amazing, wild,
wonderful grace.

Maybe you have a hard time receiving that grace for yourself. Maybe you feel dark and twisty and irredeemable inside, and you can't imagine Jesus standing in the gap for you, protecting you from your accusers. Or maybe you have a hard time showing this kind of grace to others. Maybe it seems like the world is decaying around you and you're the only one who is getting it right.

If either of those is the case for you right now, you're not alone! But let's take a close look at our Savior's example here. He treated this woman caught in adultery with dignity, kindness, and respect, even though she had done wrong. Then he followed up with important truths, spoken in love. That's how he approaches us, and that's how he wants us to approach others who need his message of repentance and redemption.

Let's take a moment to fully grab onto the idea that Jesus' grace is for us and for all those around us, even if they're struggling.

Do you ever struggle with grace, whether accepting it for yourself or extending it to others? Which of these is harder for you?

....

....

....

....

....

Martha of Bethany

"Jesus said to [Martha], 'I am the resurrection and the life. The one who believes in me will live, even though they die; and whoever lives by believing in me will never die. Do you believe this?' 'Yes, Lord,' she replied, 'I believe that you are the Messiah, the Son of God, who is to come into the world.'"
—John 11:25–27

Martha sometimes gets a bad rap. The Lord rebuked her for being too preoccupied while she was entertaining Jesus and his disciples (Luke 10:40–42). Then, Martha and her sister, Mary, lost their brother, Lazarus (John 11:19–24). Jesus was about to perform a miracle, but he was also offering one of his most devoted followers words of comfort. And frankly, her response was incredible.

Martha's confession here reveals a deeper, better, fuller understanding of Jesus' exact identity than many of the disciples had until after the crucifixion and resurrection. Martha got it.

It's sad she's often remembered *only* for her shortcoming—her bad attitude about Mary not helping her entertain at their home. Martha was so much more than that. She was undyingly practical. She was a doer. She may have cared a little too much about everything going perfectly. But her theology was sound. Her understanding of the Messiah—and her faith in him—was deep and true.

People want to put us in a box sometimes, just like they've done to Martha for centuries. It's easy to think of people as only one thing, but we're all more complex than that. We can't often control how others choose to define us. But we can make sure we don't pigeonhole people in this way. It's frustrating and unfair, so let's strive to appreciate people for all their many facets!

In your past reading, how have you felt about Martha? Do you find her practical nature and frank conversations with Jesus relatable?

....

....

....

....

....

....

....

Mary of Bethany

"When Mary reached the place where Jesus was
and saw him, she fell at his feet and said, 'Lord, if
you had been here, my brother would not have died.'
When Jesus saw her weeping, and the Jews who had
come along with her also weeping, he was deeply
moved in spirit and troubled. . . . Jesus wept."
—John 11:32–33, 35

This is one of Jesus' most tender moments recorded in the Bible. That simple verse—*Jesus wept*—is powerful, heartbreaking, and beautiful. Did it particularly move him to see Mary, Martha's sister who had sat at his feet to learn, grieve for her brother? It seems to have. Our savior was a human being, and perhaps no verse proves it better than this one.

Given that Jesus was so humanly real, with powerful emotions, isn't it strange how we sometimes expect his followers to be stoic? Sometimes Christians are expected to put on a brave face and be bold, accepting, strong, and perfect in the midst of whatever life throws at us.

Nonsense. God doesn't require that of us. He requires us to trust him. To lean on him. To let him share in our heartbrokenness the way Jesus shared in Mary's. That is the "easy yoke" Jesus puts on us—that we would rely on *his* strength, not our own. His holiness, not our own. His perfection, not our own.

Mary was not afraid to invite Jesus in to her heartbreak. She was not ashamed to allow the Savior to weep with her.

Do you struggle with feeling like you need to have complete command of your human emotions to be a "good Christian"? Do you make consistent practice of inviting Jesus in to your toughest moments?

The Widow with Two Coins

"As Jesus looked up, he saw the rich putting their gifts into the temple treasury. He also saw a poor widow put in two very small copper coins. 'Truly I tell you,' he said, 'this poor widow has put in more than all the others. All these people gave their gifts out of their wealth; but she out of her poverty put in all she had to live on.'"
—Luke 21:1–4

Here is another "nameless" woman of the New Testament who is only known by descriptors of her life (poor widow) and what she did (gave two coins). There are many others like her, as Jesus' ministry intersected with the lives of women all the time, and they're all worth reading about.

This widow is a remarkable picture of faith in God's provision. She trusted God to provide for her, so she was willing to give *all* she had. As we see from Jesus' words, the actual monetary value of what she gave was irrelevant. God can use tiny amounts of money—or even no money at all—to do great things. That wasn't the point. The point was that she had so little, but she gave *every bit of it.*

That's hard to fathom. Our culture is pretty materialistic. We like our worldly playthings. We even tend to idolize wealth and success, considering those things markers of a "blessed" life. Can you imagine giving it all over to God if he asked—not only your wealth or your playthings, but even the money you had planned to live on?

That's crazy, daring, widow-sized faith right there.

Even if God isn't asking you to give everything right this second, what is one way you can bring that spirit of wild generosity and humble sacrifice before God this week?

Mary Magdalene

"When Jesus rose early on the first day of the week, he appeared first to Mary Magdalene, out of whom he had driven seven demons."
—Mark 16:9

Mary Magdalene's reputation has gone through a millennia-long game of telephone. Through pop culture references and word-of-mouth discussion about her, she unfairly has the reputation of having been a sexually immoral woman or a professional prostitute. But the Bible doesn't say either of these things, only that Jesus cast seven demons from her.

How did her story get so mixed up? It began centuries ago when her story got mixed up with that of another unnamed woman in the Bible who was referred to as "sinful" (Luke 7:36–50). We can only imagine how Mary Magdalene might feel if she were alive today and she could see what the common perception of her is. If you have ever been the subject of an untrue rumor, you can probably relate.

Having your reputation dragged through the mud is awful. There's no getting around it. But, like Mary might if she were alive today, we can rest easy in the knowledge that God always knows the truth. No matter what anyone else's idea of us may be, God knows whether or not we fit the box we're being put in. While it's okay to defend our honor and speak the truth about ourselves, our ultimate comfort comes from the God of truth!

Have you ever been the subject of an untrue rumor or perception? What are some ways to lovingly respond to such misinformation?

....

....

....

....

....

....

....

....

Sapphira

"Now a man named Ananias, together with his wife Sapphira, also sold a piece of property. With his wife's full knowledge he kept back part of the money for himself, but brought the rest and put it at the apostles' feet."
—Acts 5:1–2

Sapphira should have been listed among our awesome early Christian women, serving alongside her husband to spread the message of Christ. Instead, we have a clear account of their deception. And that's what their sin was. It wasn't that they didn't give the full amount the field sold for. It was the fact that they lied about it. They wanted the glory associated with making a big, generous sacrifice without actually having to make the sacrifice.

In their greed and deception, Ananias and Sapphira misrepresented themselves—but they also misrepresented Jesus. Think about what kind of picture that would have presented to any unbelievers who knew what they had done—a couple who said they followed Jesus but acted untruthfully and greedily. "Hypocrite" would be the accurate word here.

It's easy to dismiss Sapphira as though she were simply a bad apple. But the deceptiveness and hypocrisy that overtook her is something everyone is vulnerable to. Even if we would never go to these lengths, it's important we present an accurate, truthful, real picture of who we are and who Jesus is through our actions. Let's guard against the spirit of Sapphira in our hearts that wants honor without sacrifice.

What are the ways you feel you most clearly, most beautifully represent Jesus to others? What are some areas you could improve upon?

Tabitha

"In Joppa there was a disciple named Tabitha
(in Greek her name is Dorcas); she was always
doing good and helping the poor."
—Acts 9:36

In the next verses, we learn that Tabitha became sick and died. Then Peter brought her back to life. But before her life became a miracle, she had this said of her: she was always doing good and helping the poor. Before she was a miracle woman, she was a living, breathing testimony to her faith.

That may sound unattainable—an entire way of life that radiates faith in Jesus as you live it. But this devotional is full of inspiration for small steps we can take toward that kind of living testimonial. There are countless other books—Bible studies, history books, the writings of theologians, and other devotionals—to help us meet this goal too.

Sit for a moment and ponder one thing—just one thing you can change to help you live as a walking, breathing testimony of your faith. Is it something to add to your life, like serving the hungry in your community? Or is it something God wants you to remove from your life, like a bad habit or an unhealthy attitude? Focus on that one thing for the next week. You'd be surprised the big changes you can make in your living testimony by taking small steps.

What is your "one thing," and what are the small practical steps you can take to work on your one thing this week?

....

....

....

....

....

....

....

....

....

....

Rhoda

"Peter knocked at the outer entrance, and a
servant named Rhoda came to answer the door.
When she recognized Peter's voice, she was so
overjoyed she ran back without opening it and
exclaimed, 'Peter is at the door!' 'You're out of your
mind,' they told her. When she kept insisting that
it was so, they said, 'It must be his angel.'"

—Acts 12:13–15

Peter had been miraculously delivered from prison. The believers gathered inside the house of Mary, mother of John Mark,
had been praying for just such a miracle. James, the brother of
John, had recently been executed, so those gathered at Mary's house
must have been praying fervently for Peter's life to be spared. And
yet, when the servant girl Rhoda bounded in to tell them who she
heard at the door—comically forgetting to let Peter inside in the
process—they didn't believe her!

We don't get much information about Rhoda. What was her

relationship like with her employer? Was she a believer too? We can suppose she heard a lot of powerful teaching as a member of that particular household. But we do know Rhoda had the faith and courage to share what she knew to be true. She was certain she recognized Peter's voice, and even though the others called her crazy, she wouldn't back down from what she knew. God had performed the miracle they'd been asking for.

Rhoda's bravery is inspirational. Not everyone will understand you, your faith, or the truth you try to share with them. But when you do these things in love with the purpose of advancing God's kingdom, you can have the boldness and steadfastness of Rhoda, no matter what anyone else thinks.

Would you consider yourself a courageous or bold person? In what ways might those qualities be helpful in your walk with God?

....

....

....

....

....

....

....

Lydia

"One of those listening was a woman from the city of Thyatira named Lydia, a dealer in purple cloth. She was a worshiper of God. The Lord opened her heart to respond to Paul's message. When she and the members of her household were baptized, she invited us to her home. 'If you consider me a believer in the Lord,' she said, 'come and stay at my house.' And she persuaded us."
—Acts 16:14–15

That's a cool tagline: *She was a worshiper of God.* And it's an even cooler description of how it feels to understand the message of Jesus for the first time: *The Lord opened her heart to respond.*

That's the message of Christianity, isn't it? God reaches down to us and gives us new eyes to see and new hearts to understand this crazy, loving thing he did for us when he sent his son to Earth. Maybe we didn't get it the first time we heard the message. But at some point, the Lord opened our hearts, and we *understood.* Lydia was one of *billions* who have heard this message. You are too. When that message touched her heart, she responded in kind and opened up her home to the disciples.

A strong desire to serve is one of the hallmarks of a newly kindled heart for Jesus. Is that the stage you're in right now? Or maybe you've been following Jesus a long time—maybe for decades—and that fire has quieted a little. It's easy to let our faith become routine. But we can always reignite the desire to serve that burned in us when we first came to know Jesus.

What were the ways you loved to serve when you first came to know Jesus? Have they changed over the years?

Priscilla

"There he met a Jew named Aquila, a native of Pontus,
who had recently come from Italy with his wife Priscilla,
because Claudius had ordered all Jews to leave Rome.
Paul went to see them." "[Later, Paul wrote,] 'Greet
Priscilla and Aquila, my co-workers in Christ Jesus.
They risked their lives for me. Not only I but all the
churches of the Gentiles are grateful to them.'"
—Acts 18:2; Romans 16:3–4

Priscilla and Aquila were some of the apostle Paul's greatest helpers. They often worked alongside him. This couple meant a lot to Paul, and as he said in his own words, he wasn't the only one who was grateful for them!

Priscilla is almost always mentioned in the same breath as her husband. That's not because she wasn't accomplished on her own (or vice versa). It's because they always worked side by side for the church.

There's an old saying that goes, "Many hands make light work."

When the burden of labor is shared, it isn't too overwhelming for any one person. How much more so when your fellow workers are beautifully in sync with a common vision, strong shared values, and a close personal relationship with one another.

Priscilla and Aquila are a wonderful example of such a dynamic team working together harmoniously. This is a cool example for working in ministry, whether with a spouse or a friend, but it also applies to other types of work, such as community service, your place of employment . . . even family projects around the house. Working in groups or with a partner can require an extra dose of patience at times. But we can accomplish more in unified teams than we ever could on our own.

Is there someone in your life with whom you partner particularly well? Perhaps you work well with certain people on certain types of projects and other people on other types of projects. What are some big goals you might accomplish with your dynamic partner(s)?

....

....

....

....

....

....

Phoebe

"I commend to you our sister Phoebe, a deacon of the church in Cenchreae. I ask you to receive her in the Lord in a way worthy of his people and to give her any help she may need from you, for she has been the benefactor of many people, including me."
—Romans 16:1–2

Phoebe began Paul's list of personal greetings as he signed his letter to the Roman church. Phoebe was called "deacon," a word which, in New Testament contexts, is usually understood to mean someone who served in that specific leadership role in the church. She likely held a formal office within the local church.

As a benefactor of many, she was probably a woman of means. She is thought by historians to be the one Paul entrusted to deliver his letter to the Romans.

Would it surprise Phoebe to know she's the subject of modern controversy about her role in the early church? Would it shock her to learn how many people know her name? In this age of social media, it's easier than ever to be "seen" by hundreds, thousands, and even millions of people. If you've ever posted something that's gotten a lot of attention, you might be able to relate to Phoebe. Everyone has an opinion about who you are, and most of them don't even know you.

We can't control others' comments, but we can be like Phoebe. We can work diligently for the Lord, we can build our reputations in the ways that matter, and we can be generous with our resources.

What are some qualities you can cultivate in your life to help you grow a reputation as a trusted sister in Christ?

Junia, Tryphena, Tryphosa, & Persis

"Greet Andronicus and Junia, my fellow Jews who have been in prison with me. They are outstanding among the apostles, and they were in Christ before I was. . . . Greet Tryphena and Tryphosa, those women who work hard in the Lord. Greet my dear friend Persis, another woman who has worked very hard in the Lord."
—Romans 16:7, 12

These four women were also included in Paul's list of greetings sent to the Roman church. If Phoebe's church leadership role is controversial, Junia's position is doubly so.

The Greek translated here "outstanding among the apostles," implying that both Andronicus and his wife, Junia, were apostles, can also be translated "well known to the apostles," implying the apostles were aware of them, but they were not themselves apostles. Both are reasonable translations, and we get no other information about Junia, except what early church fathers said about her (which lands on the side of "among the apostles").

And then there are Tryphena and Tryphosa, "who work[ed] hard in the Lord," and Persis, a "woman who has worked very hard in the Lord."

These female church leaders, examples, and servants have one thing in common—they *did work* for Jesus and his church. Their specific types of service varied. Their specific roles varied. But whatever they were called to do, and whatever God put before them, they did it.

What a tremendous example for us. There is never a shortage of work to be done when it comes to caring for the vulnerable members of society, encouraging believers, and sharing the gospel. Let's follow the example of these great women who came before us.

What are a few things you could do over the next week to serve the Lord beyond your usual ministries? What if you expanded that timeline to the next year?

Eunice & Lois

"I am reminded of your sincere faith, which first lived
in your grandmother Lois and in your mother Eunice
and, I am persuaded, now lives in you also."
—2 Timothy 1:5

It's fitting that our final biblical ladies are Eunice, the mother of Timothy, and Lois, his grandmother. Timothy was Paul's pastor protégé, and Paul's letters to him are full of excellent pastoral advice. But he opened his second letter with a personal note about Timothy's lineage. We know from Acts 16:1 that Eunice was a Jewish believer and Timothy's father was Greek. Both of the maternal figures in Timothy's life poured faithfulness into their boy, and he grew up to have "sincere faith." Eunice and Lois passed it on.

We don't grow in godliness and stretch our faithfulness only for our own well-being. That's a great benefit, sure. As we build up the church, we're built up too. But we're also looking to pass along a legacy of faith to others. Maybe we'll pass it along to our actual children and grandchildren. Maybe we'll be like spiritual parents through mentorship. Or maybe our legacy will be written in a book or online, and we won't even meet those who are changed by our words. Each of us will leave something behind—a legacy of the life we lived and what mattered to us most.

How do you want to be remembered? If you could pass on one thing to the next generation, what would it be?

God's Heart for You

"There is neither Jew nor Gentile, neither
slave nor free, nor is there male and female,
for you are all one in Christ Jesus."
—Galatians 3:28

Paul didn't write these words to erase cultural identity. He didn't write them to erase masculinity or femininity. God created different people groups with specific, unique beauty. And he created men and women equally reflective of his character. Paul wasn't trying to undo that with his statement here. No, he was highlighting a rich truth: whatever the differences between people on Earth—different languages, cultures, backstories, economic situations, life experiences, or genders—we are all one in Jesus.

This is an amazing message. Sometimes women are oppressed, especially in certain cultures and in certain eras past. We've made great strides toward equality. Words like *agency*, *consent*, and *empowerment* are part of our cultural conversation now. But thousands of years ago, God revealed *his* view: women have always mattered to him, and we have always been a valuable part of his church, an important part of his plan.

Be empowered, beloved sister, because you were created to be an on-fire-for-God, kingdom-building woman. We've seen stories of women whose lives are cautionary tales. But we've also seen dozens of examples of godly women living out their callings from God. Let's walk in their footsteps and be the women we were created to be!

What is something unique about the way God created you, and how might *you* use the very specific *you* God created to serve him in your life?

From the Publisher

GREAT BOOKS

ARE EVEN BETTER WHEN THEY'RE SHARED!

Help other readers find this one:

- Post a review at your favorite online bookseller

- Post a picture on a social media account and share why you enjoyed it

- Send a note to a friend who would also love it—or better yet, give them a copy

Thanks for reading!